Earthquake

Perspectives on Earthquake Disasters

Anne Rooney

capstone

To contact Capstone Global Library, please call 800-747-4992, or visit our web site www.capstonepub.com

Edited by Andrew Farrow, James Benefield, and Claire Throp
Designed by Philippa Jenkins
Original illustrations © Capstone Global Library Ltd 2014
Picture research by Tracy Cummins
Originated by Capstone Global Library Ltd

Library of Congress Cataloging-in-Publication Data
Rooney, Anne.
  Earthquake : perspectives on earthquake disasters / Anne Rooney.—First edition.
    pages cm.—(Disaster dossiers)
  Includes bibliographical references and index.
  ISBN 978-1-4846-0180-8 (hb)—ISBN 978-1-4846-0186-0 (pb) 1. Earthquakes—Juvenile literature. I. Title.

  QE521.3.R663 2015
  363.34'95—dc23   2013041058

Acknowledgments
We would like to thank the following for permission to reproduce photographs: Corbis pp. 16 (© Niko Guido), 18 (© Christophe Calais); Defenseimagery.mil pp. 4 (MCCS Spike Call), 10 (U.S. Navy photo by Mass Communication Specialist 2nd Class John Stratton); Getty Images pp. 6 (Shaul Schwartz), 12 (Logan Abassi/AFP), 14, 15 (Paul J. Richards/AFP), 21 (Sophia Paris/Minustah), 23 (Antonio Bolfo), 25, 28, 31 (Stan Honda/AFP), 26, 32, 47 (Thony Belizaire/AFP), 27 (Alberto E. Rodriguez), 39 (Martin Bernetti/AFP), 41 (Niels Busch), 44 (Belizaire/AFP), 48 (Yoshikazu Tsuno/AFP); Newscom p. 9 (AFP Photo/Stan Honda); Shutterstock p. 22 (Maksim Kabakou); U.S. Department of Defense p. 33 (Fred W. Baker III); U.S. Navy photo pp. 38 (Air crewman 2nd Class Shawn), 49 (Mass Communication Specialist 1st Class Joshua Lee Kelsey).

Cover photograph of rescuers checking a collapsed building after an earthquake in April 2013 in the Lingguan township in Yaan, Sichuan province, southwest China, reproduced with permission of Getty Images (STR/AFP).

Every effort has been made to contact copyright holders of material reproduced in this book. Any omissions will be rectified in subsequent printings if notice is given to the publisher.

Disclaimer
All the Internet addresses (URLs) given in this book were valid at the time of going to press. However, due to the dynamic nature of the Internet, some addresses may have changed, or sites may have changed or ceased to exist since publication. While the author and publisher regret any inconvenience this may cause readers, no responsibility for any such changes can be accepted by either the author or the publisher.

Printed in the United States of America.
112018   001276

Contents

Some words are printed in bold, **like this**. You can find out
what they mean by looking in the glossary.

DOSSIER:
THE HAITI EARTHQUAKE

On January 12, 2010, the strongest earthquake to strike Haiti since 1770 destroyed most of the buildings in the capital, Port-au-Prince, and the surrounding countryside. The quake also tore up roads and bridges. Hundreds of thousands of people were killed or injured and millions were left homeless. Roads, airports, and seaports were closed, and power and phone lines were broken. The country was left without effective government or emergency services.

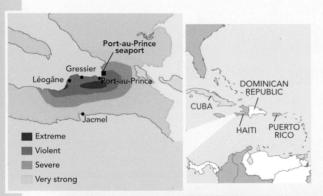

Port-au-Prince seaport

Gressier

Léogâne

Port-au-Prince

Jacmel

■ Extreme
■ Violent
■ Severe
□ Very strong

DOMINICAN REPUBLIC

CUBA

HAITI

PUERTO RICO

Haiti occupies the western third of the island of Hispaniola in the Caribbean, off the coast of Central America. The Dominican Republic occupies the rest of the island. The earthquake hit densely populated areas.

Damage to Port-au-Prince is seen here from the air, on January 30, 2010.

∨

TIME OF EVENT:	4:53:09 p.m., local time, January 12, 2010
DURATION:	15–20 seconds
MAGNITUDE (SEE PAGE 37):	7.0
AFTERSHOCKS:	two of magnitude 6.0 and 5.5 within minutes; 59 aftershocks of magnitude 4.5 or above by February 23
EPICENTER:	15 mi. (25 km) WSW of Port-au-Prince
CASUALTIES:	around 300,000 dead, 196,000 injured
DAMAGE IN PORT-AU-PRINCE:	190,000 houses badly damaged, 105,000 completely destroyed; 1.5 million people homeless. Most school, government, and administrative buildings destroyed.

FIRST DAYS TIMELINE

JANUARY 12, 4:53:09 p.m.
U.S. Geological Survey (USGS) announces the earthquake.

JANUARY 13, 12:00:00 p.m.
A damage-assessment team starts work from the U.S. embassy in Port-au-Prince.
Two hospitals start treating the wounded.
U.S. Coast Guard helicopters fly over Haiti to assess the situation.
Aid teams arrive from Dominican Republic, Cuba, and Peru.
U.S. Air Force Combat Controllers set up an air-traffic control system at Port-au-Prince airport.

JANUARY 14
More than 20 countries send aid.
The Port-au-Prince morgue is overwhelmed by large numbers of dead bodies.

The Day Earth Broke

On January 12, 2010, the citizens of Port-au-Prince were going about their daily business. Then the earthquake struck. Within seconds, their lives were turned upside down and their city was destroyed. Poorly built concrete homes crashed down, burying their occupants. Schools, hospitals, government buildings, and the president's palace shook apart and crumbled. The streets were torn up and filled with debris. Hundreds of thousands of people were hurt or killed. The air filled with choking dust from smashed concrete. One witness said Port-au-Prince was "nothing but a mass of rubble, overshadowed by a vast cloud of dust which hides the city from the sky." The city was a scene of total devastation.

Frightened, injured, and confused people crowded the streets. They wandered aimlessly or sat near their destroyed homes. No one knew where to go for help.

Getting outside

Everyone who could escape ran out into the streets, afraid of more **tremors** and desperate to leave buildings that might collapse at any moment. Many more were trapped inside, some pinned under the tangle of metal and concrete. Terrified and injured survivors began searching for loved ones or help. Charity worker Rachmani Domersant saw "thousands of people sitting in the streets with nowhere to go…people running, crying, screaming."

Trapped

Survivors trapped under rubble had no idea whether they would be found. They lay in darkness, often in pain, listening to the panic around them. Some called out, tapped on the concrete, or tried to use their cell phones to alert rescuers. People above scrambled over broken slabs of concrete, clawing through the rubble with their hands to try to free trapped family and friends. Meanwhile, frightening aftershocks brought down more buildings and shifted the rubble.

The moment the quake struck

"After the roaring, the rumbling, and the crashing stopped, there was crying, horror, and unimaginable scenes all around us."

Matt Marek, from the Red Cross

"Our truck was being tossed to and fro like a toy, and when it stopped, I looked out of the windows to see buildings pancaking down… We piled bodies into the back of our truck, and took them down the hill with us, hoping to find medical attention… It took about two hours to go less than one mile."

Bob Poff, from the Salvation Army

No help

The disaster also crippled the emergency services, leaving no effective police, ambulance, or fire service. The government and the **United Nations (UN)** mission in Haiti were both badly hit. While there was already a large UN presence in Haiti, without orders coming from headquarters, local UN commanders focused on controlling **looting** and were slow to shift to **humanitarian** aid.

People could not understand why help did not come. Alastair Cameron, a British citizen working in Haiti at the time, wondered why the UN did nothing: "[There were] a huge number of UN personnel in position. They could have started to distribute food and water, but they did nothing... I find it hard to believe that senior officers...could not have acted on their own and shown a little initiative."

Port-au-Prince resident Henry Narces said, "There is nothing, nothing at all, no aid. It's an abomination, all the world can see what is happening but we have no help. We are left to help each other."

Comfort in God

Haitians are religious people— around 80 percent are Roman Catholic.

"Church groups are singing throughout the city all through the night in prayer. It is a beautiful sound in the middle of a horrible tragedy."

Tweeted by Troy Livesay, a U.S. **missionary** living in Haiti

An expatriate's perspective

Expatriate Christine Blanchard lives in the United States. She worried about her family in Haiti:

"My family is still missing. The phone lines are down and I haven't been able to get in touch with them...It's just so awful. I feel sick with worry. I am devastated...I have been up all night."

Darkness falls

Broken electricity cables started fires that glowed as night fell. Otherwise it was pitch black, with no electric lights or streetlights. No one dared go into buildings for shelter—there were eight aftershocks during the first night, and weakened buildings might fall down. Regina Tauschek, working in Port-au-Prince with the German aid agency Welthungerhilfe, said:

"The dead are lying in the streets, thousands of people are spending the night outdoors. They are lacking absolutely everything: water, food, medical care."

The world gets to hear of it

With no landline phones operating in the earthquake zone, the world first heard about the disaster through cell phone and Twitter messages from those on the ground (see page 22).

But even before specific details of the quake were confirmed, the international response began. The International Red Cross (IRC) loaded planes with supplies for Haiti. The International Medical Corps landed its first emergency team in Haiti 22 hours after the earthquake. The day after the quake, a team from the U.S. Air Force arrived to open the destroyed airport at Port-au-Prince and run air-traffic control so that planes carrying relief supplies could land. The world began to help.

People hunt through the rubble of Port-au-Prince looking for anything that might be useful. They have lost their homes and possessions.

Emergency!

When a major disaster happens, the international community responds quickly. The first stage of response is to rescue people. The next is relief of suffering. The last—and longest—stage is to aid the recovery.

First response

Within hours of hearing about the quake, governments around the world promised to give money, food, and medical aid. They sent **search and rescue teams** and military assistance to help keep order, provide medical help, clear rubble, and distribute supplies. Within 24 hours, the UN World Food Program—which was already in Haiti—began distributing food to affected people.

The first teams to arrive were from the United States, Peru, and Cuba, countries geographically close to Haiti. Two Peruvian Air Force planes took over 50 tons of food and rescue teams to help search for survivors. James Sweetman arrived on January 14 with the U.S. Coast Guard: "The first few days we were taking tree branches and breaking them for splints. We cut wool blankets for slings and made backboards [stretchers] out of doors."

A U.S. Coast Guard helicopter takes people injured in the earthquake to get treatment elsewhere.

Help on the ground

Haiti is a poor country that has suffered much hardship. Many aid organizations and the UN already had operations there. Although the quake hit the offices of **nongovernment organizations (NGOs)** in Haiti, their presence meant they could start coordinating the rescue and relief work.

One Red Cross clinic was badly damaged, but local people who saw the Red Cross sign still came for help. Workers spent all night cleaning and bandaging wounds and sent emergency teams out into the city to help. They carried out triage—assessing people's injuries and deciding how they should be treated—and organized a basic health care unit.

Local help: Thomas's story

Thomas Oronti lives in the Dominican Republic, Haiti's island neighbor. The weekend after the earthquake, he and his coworkers drove with food and water to Port-au-Prince. He saw a different side of the relief effort:

"I am surprised there weren't more people handing out aid...The NGOs will eventually distribute their aid but they are taking too long and a direct response is needed now. The Haitian people need to know someone cares, and at the moment no way near enough is being done to give out that message."

Help not needed

When a massive earthquake struck Sichuan province, China, on May 12, 2008, killing over 69,000 people, the Chinese government turned down offers of foreign help. China has a history of devastating earthquakes and has considerable expertise in dealing with search and rescue and aid missions. The government believed it was able to cope with the disaster without outside help. However, the UN and several other nations provided support later on.

Nicolette, a nurse, was cooking when the earthquake struck. She went straight to the hospital when she realized what had happened: "There was nothing to work with. No power, no **sanitary items**, no gloves…I had to use whatever I could to clean the wounds. We organized ourselves with what we had and helped the people who were in the hospital."

DOSSIER:
HAITI

Haiti is the poorest country in the western **hemisphere**. Over 70 percent of the population live on less than $2 a day, and 50 percent lives on less than $1 a day. At the time of the earthquake, much of Port-au-Prince's population lived in tightly packed, poorly built **slums**. Many people were unemployed or sold goods and food on the streets. Fewer than half of the children attended school, while 225,000 children worked as unpaid servants (modern slaves). There was no sewage system—waste flowed in ditches down the streets.

∨ This was the National Palace, home of the president, in Port-au-Prince before the earthquake in January 2010.

∧ This is the palace a few days after the earthquake.

HAITI TIMELINE

1492
Spain claims Hispaniola. By 1514, most of the native Taíno Indians die.

1697
Hispaniola is divided between France and Spain

1791
Slave rebellion challenges French rulers

1804
Haiti becomes the first black-led **republic** in the world

1825
Recognized by France; a long, unstable period of semi-independence follows

1915–1934
U.S. occupation of Haiti

1957–1971/1971–1986
Brutal reign of presidents "Doc" François Duvalier and then his son "Bébé Doc"

1986–2004
Fragile, unstable **democracy**

2004
President Aristide overthrown.
UN peacekeepers arrived to try to stabilize the country.

Checking the situation

An effective rescue and relief operation begins with an assessment of the full extent of the disaster. But delays cost lives, so the assessment took place alongside the initial relief work. Google Earth posted updated photos of Haiti the day after the earthquake to help disaster relief workers. The U.S. Air Force carried out **reconnaissance** from the air. An international team of engineers on the ground inspected the city's buildings. This type of preparation is necessary to run a safe rescue operation. It helps teams decide what equipment to send where, and which roads are still passable or need to be cleared.

Hard to rescue

Only one road was open from the airport to Port-au-Prince, and it took a day to travel it. In the city, the roads were narrow, crowded, and blocked with rubble. This made it difficult to move rescue teams and equipment into the area, and they struggled to operate when they arrived.

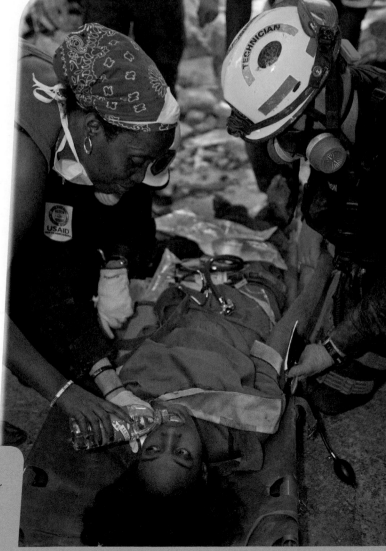

Rescue workers give student Mikila Foster her first drink of water. She had been buried under rubble for 72 hours.

DOSSIER:
THE NEW YORK URBAN SEARCH AND RESCUE TASK FORCE, K-9 UNIT

The K-9 (canine) unit is a team of 74 officers, plus dogs, from police and fire departments in New York City. The team leader for the Haiti mission was Fire Chief Joe Downey. The team got the call to leave for Haiti at 2 a.m. on January 14 and left New York at 1 p.m. They arrived late because of delays at the airport in Haiti, but they spent a week in the country, pulling six survivors from the rubble—three of them within hours of arriving. They worked at a different site each day.

QUICK FACTS

PLACE OF TRAINING:	Two specially built "disaster zone" sites on Staten Island, New York
TIME SPENT DOG TRAINING:	600 hours per dog
DOG'S JOB:	To locate people beneath rubble—it only responds to the smell of living survivors

Left with even less

"[The] devastation is unimaginable...These towns we went to—there was nothing, nothing left to be rebuilt...People down there had...very little to start with. Now they have nothing. They're living in the streets. They're living in parks."

Joe Downey, fire chief, K-9 unit

In Haiti, 211 people were rescued by search and rescue teams. More people were pulled out of the rubble by their neighbors; these are not all included in official figures.

Finding People in the Rubble

At first, survivors used shovels, hammers, and bare hands to tackle towering piles of rubble. Iyvel Muresu tried to dig people out from under an office building: "Since yesterday, we have been trying to save people, but the ground is still trembling. They have been asking for water and hitting things to make noise, but we don't have the ability to save them."

Better buildings

When a powerful earthquake struck Sendai, Japan, in 2011, better building standards led to fewer deaths: around 1,000 people were killed. (More died in the tsunami that happened after the quake.) Buildings in Japan are designed to withstand earthquakes. The buildings will bend and sway rather than fall, giving people time to escape.

Backhoes and **hydraulic jacks** are used to move large slabs that might be covering spaces—known as **voids**—where survivors could be found. The concrete slabs protected people from further harm by providing a "roof."

On January 15, 25 rescue teams from eight countries were on site—two days later, that number had risen to 40, comprising 1,800 rescue workers and more than 160 dogs. They asked local people's advice on finding survivors, the best routes through the city, and how the buildings were constructed.

Difficult recovery

Evans Monsignac lay buried in rubble for 27 days. He survived by sipping sewage water that leaked through the ground above him. He was rescued and taken to Florida for treatment, but he was scared that the doctors and nurses were going to kill him. Dr. David Smith treated Monsignac and said: "If he was from the U.S. we would put a tube down his nose to feed him, but in Haitian culture if they have a tube like that it implies that they are going to die. When he first came in, we put 12 tubes in him in eight hours and he pulled them all out, screaming from the psychological trauma." He explained that Monsignac was convinced that his mother had sold him to white slave traders and he would be a slave for the rest of his life. It took patience and understanding to persuade Monsignac that he was in safe hands.

Hi-tech search and rescue

Search and rescue teams used sophisticated equipment to find people under the rubble.
- Thermal imaging cameras show the warmth of a living body.
- Video cameras on a flexible pole are pushed through gaps in the rubble.
- Microphones are pushed into spaces. Rescuers tap and pick up any response with the microphone. Some microphones can pick up a heartbeat.
- Carbon dioxide meters pushed into spaces detect raised levels of carbon dioxide where a survivor is breathing.

Every rescue is different

For every successful rescue, there is a rescued survivor and one or more rescuers. But not all rescues are successful. The job brings joy and sorrow. For survivors, too, it can be a time of grief if they discover a family member has died. Not everyone can be rescued. At the Hotel Montana, rescuers heard one voice from under the rubble call, "Go help other people. There's no way you can help me."

Survivor: Kiki's story

Kiki Joachin was playing at home while his mother, Odinel, cooked dinner. Suddenly, bricks and plaster started to fall on him and his sister as the six-story building collapsed. Odinel thought Kiki and his sister were dead. But a week later, Kiki's aunt heard him calling out,

"Mama! Help us, Mama! Water!"

She found a crew of police officers and firefighters from New York. They dug for hours and finally punched holes through the debris covering Kiki and his small sister, lifting them to safety.

French rescue workers pull two girls from the rubble, where they had been trapped for two days.

Rescuer: Jose's story

Jose Medina is a firefighter from Florida. He went to Haiti as part of a team of 70 volunteers. The team worked on freeing people trapped in a collapsed supermarket. They began planning their search by looking at photos of how the supermarket was built, to figure out what the inside might be like. They had to make their way through five stories, heaps of concrete, and the food, clothes, and other items sold in the supermarket.

"There are a lot of unstable things. We don't know if this building was built the way it was supposed to be built,"

he said. They turned off their cutting equipment to talk to the trapped people. Medina had only eaten high-energy snack bars since arriving in Haiti, and he hadn't slept. The families of the people trapped stood around the edge of the work area, anxious but unable to do anything except wait.

Parent: Manushka's story

Not every rescue is successful. Manushka spent four days trying to get someone to dig her 10-year-old daughter from the wreckage of a daycare center. The Los Angeles County Fire Search and Rescue Team heard tapping sounds and tried for several hours with rescue dogs to locate her. Eventually the tapping stopped. The dogs found no sign of life, and the team pulled out to help people at another site. A journalist saw Manushka as the team left:

"It was a heartbreaking scene as the lights were pulled down, the crews drove off, to see that mother sitting silently, praying for some sort of miracle, for something that will bring her daughter back to life."

Think about this

If you were a disaster manager and you managed a search and rescue team, how would you set priorities for digging people out of the rubble? How could you choose which people to rescue first?

Dealing with the dead

The large number of dead bodies overwhelmed the city's morgues. Many were collected in trucks and buried in mass graves or burned because they would rot quickly in the heat. By January 23, 75,000 bodies had been buried in 12 large trenches.

People often fear that leaving bodies unburied will lead to disease, but public health expert Steven Rottman explained, "The risk of dead bodies following natural disasters being a source for spreading infectious diseases is very, very small." The World Health Organization (WHO) recommended corpses should be treated with chemicals and buried in open ditches so that relatives had a chance to identify them. But another public health expert, Linda Degutis, thinks mass graves are sometimes best: "It's probably far more disturbing to have a lot of dead bodies laying around that aren't being moved and buried."

Helping the spirit

The mass disposal of bodies upset local people, who saw it as desecration (insulting to the dead). Both the medical charities Red Cross and Doctors Without Borders spoke out against mass burials. Psychiatrist Lynne Jones warned, "If deaths are not dignified—that is, lacking proper burials or mourning ceremonies—this denies people the means to accept and come to terms with their loss." Most Haitians are Catholics, but half also have **voodoo** beliefs. A canzo, or voodoo nurse, helps the spirit on its way. "The spirits are not in peace and that is painful," one canzo said. "Where will they go? Where will their spirits go?" Haiti's chief voodoo priest, Max Beauvoir, explained the impact: "The Haitian people are wounded. They are not just wounded in their body alone, they are wounded in their spirit."

Visions of hell

Mati Goldstein, head of the Israeli ZAKA International Rescue Unit, found the number of dead overwhelming:

"Everywhere, the acrid smell of bodies hangs in the air. It's just like the stories we are told of the **Holocaust**—thousands of bodies everywhere. You have to understand that the situation is true madness, and the more time passes, there are more and more bodies, in numbers that cannot be grasped. It is beyond comprehension."

Workers take unidentified bodies to a mass grave outside Port-au-Prince.

Telling the World

The first accounts of the disaster emerged from Haiti through social networking sites and by text message, long before foreign journalists reached the scene.

First reports

At 5:12 p.m., around 19 minutes after the first tremor, the USGS issued an international alert about the earthquake.

The first photographs of the earthquake zone were taken on cell phones and posted on Twitpic, and the first film footage was posted on YouTube by Oxfam at 10 p.m., just four hours after the quake. Facebook reported 1,500 status updates every minute containing the word "Haiti."

> Heavy earthquake right now! In Haiti
> (Fredo Dupoux on Twitter, 5:00 p.m.)

Viral news

News of the earthquake followed the same pattern seen in other major disasters in recent years: unofficial information from those on the ground spread around the world before official news channels or government bodies had anything to say. The mainstream **media** and even the Haitian government and UN were silent while the Internet buzzed with informal firsthand reports.

January 12, 2010 21:53:09

(Mw 7.0) Haiti Region. 10 miles (16 km) SW (227 degrees) of Port-au-Prince, Haiti.

TWITTER TIMELINE: Richard Morse's story

Richard Morse runs a hotel in Haiti and is a musician and writer. He sent messages throughout the days following the earthquake.

Tuesday, January 12

6:23 p.m.: A lot of big buildings in PaP [Port-au-Prince] are down!

6:39 p.m.: People are bringing people by on stretchers

7:45 p.m.: Another aftershock...people are screaming and freaking out down towards the stadium...much singing and praying in large numbers

10:11 p.m.: It's getting quieter in PaP...no helicopters, no sound of ambulances

Wednesday, January 13

12:38 p.m.: I saw a couple of helicopters twice today, but there is no sign that the international presence is helping the population

12:56 p.m.: I am hearing the siren of an ambulance for the first time

1:24 p.m.: I see bodies in the street...buried in rubble, decomposing bodies

6:00 p.m.: People that came in from the airport are saying that there are bodies strewn about on the streets. I don't know what to make of that.

6:14 p.m.: Bodies are being put by the side of the Canape Vert road so friends and relatives can come pick them up

6:47 p.m.: I hear help is coming...tomorrow

8:55 p.m.: Night has fallen...The night seems to take so long...I guess those that are buried alive in the rubble are feeling it the worst...Prayers

Saturday, January 16

8:23 a.m.: WHO'S IN CHARGE?

Into the mainstream

Before the mainstream media could get journalists to Haiti, they used social media. The *Los Angeles Times* created a list of users tweeting from Haiti, while the *New York Times* asked for people on the ground to update their news blog. The news channel CNN encouraged people in Haiti to upload their own photos and videos, which became CNN's main source of material in the first days after the earthquake.

Being wary

Although these sources provided immediate and **graphic** glimpses into the situation on the ground, they were not always reliable and could not show the bigger picture. Some stories were even made up—at one point, someone posted film from an earthquake in Japan, claiming it showed Haiti's earthquake. A report that the UN's World Food Program food store had been looted later turned out to be false. Georgia Popplewell, managing director of the international blogging network Global Voices, warned, "It's difficult to verify information…but in the end you'll see only a tiny fraction of the whole, and perhaps understand or read accurately only a fraction of that."

Journalists move in

The first official reports from Haiti were from local journalists and overseas journalists already stationed in the country. More soon arrived, first from nearby countries, including the United States. Their reports were more objective than the personal stories on the Internet. But journalists faced considerable problems, from lack of electricity to struggles with transportation and supplies. There was also a language barrier—most Haitians speak Haitian Creole, a language related to French but not spoken outside Haiti.

Journalists in trouble

Some regimes keep tight control of the media and manage the public image of disasters. The Chinese writer Huang Qi was jailed for three years after investigating **corruption**. He said it led to poor building standards in Sichuan, causing the deaths of children when schools collapsed in an earthquake in 2008. He was refused permission to enter the area when an earthquake struck Sichuan in 2013.

A voice for Haitians

When officials failed to deliver on promises, when camps were badly run, and when aid didn't get to those who needed it, the media also helped Haitians to tell the world of their suffering. When stories of looting and other crimes started to appear, Haitian journalist Ansel Herz answered back: "I have not seen a single incidence of violence. The tent camps through the city…are destitute but totally peaceful… Tell CNN, the BBC, and other media to stop being alarmist fear-mongers." In reality, looting was a serious problem in some areas, but rare or nonexistent in others (see page 30).

Official messages

After an earthquake in Christchurch, New Zealand, on February 22, 2011, the *New Zealand Herald* and New Zealand government's official earthquake Twitter account, CEQgovtnz, kept the country informed in the aftermath of the disaster.

Camera crews film in a hospital in Port-au-Prince, reporting on the disaster.

The media and the world

You might think that journalists covering a disaster get in the way and use up essential resources. But people outside the area want to know what is happening. Those with friends and relatives in Haiti were desperate for any news. Haitians also needed information on where to find medical attention, shelter, food, and water, how to trace loved ones, and what to do with dead bodies.

The media and aid

The public often judges the importance of a disaster by the amount of news coverage it gets. This prompts people to **donate** to the charities helping on the ground. This then spurs on businesses, corporations, and governments to give money. But as the story of the earthquake became old news, and the media's attention moved elsewhere, donations started to slow down. Some aid organizations also feared that the stories about looting (see page 30) made people not want to donate.

A technician installs a satellite dish outside the destroyed presidential palace the day after the earthquake.

Movie stars such as Leonardo di Caprio and Sean Penn encouraged people to donate.

The media began publicizing charity appeals and running advertisements for donations free of charge. Each time they showed another survivor being pulled from the rubble, or the suffering of those in camps or **field hospitals**, people were reminded to give money. Instant ways of giving—such as by text message—allowed people to donate more easily. The American Red Cross raised $3 million within 24 hours through a campaign using text messages.

A journalist's perspective

"The days are scorching hot, water is in scarce supply, the sanitation situation is dire. People in the streets were opening manhole covers to wash themselves using the water in the pipes below, and long lines have formed at every gas station, with people stocking up on fuel in case they need to escape."

Christina Boyle, U.S. journalist

A skeptic's perspective

Some critics have suggested that the victims of the Haiti earthquake were themselves responsible for the much of the disaster. U.S. blogger and ex-basketball player Paul Shirley wrote: "I haven't donated a cent to the Haitian relief effort. And I probably will not...I don't think the people of Haiti will do much with my money...Shouldn't much of the *responsibility* for the disaster lie with the victims of that disaster?... It is not the responsibility of the outside world to provide help...especially when people choose to influence their own existences negatively." Shirley lost his job with sports broadcaster ESPN as a result of these comments.

Rescue to Relief

After the immediate rescue operation ended, the need for food, shelter, water, and medical assistance continued. The relief effort would last for years.

Food aid

Many people in Haiti had too little to eat even before the earthquake. Afterward, with stores and markets destroyed or closed, hunger became an urgent problem. Two million people were in need of food. In the countryside, people began to starve. Elin Plantin, a 65-year-old woman living at Gressier refugee camp, said, "Since the earthquake, I don't have much more than one cup of coffee a day. There is no money and nowhere to get hold of any food and water either."

Foreign governments, large NGOs such as the World Food Program, and charities rushed emergency food rations to Haiti. The very first food aid was high-energy cookies. These keep people alive and are easy to store and transport. After the first few days, shipments of normal food arrived, with cooking pots and other items so that people could cook.

A United Nations unit distributes water and food to Haitians as part of the earthquake relief.

A mother's perspective

Clotide Anilus and her family depended on food provided by Oxfam. She got four plates of food a day to share among her family of five.

"This community canteen is what is left for my family and me to survive. I have never been able to get any tickets giving access to the distribution of food items because it's not well organized, which complicates things for me with my three children and sick husband...We manage to share a dish between the two of us. Not a big deal, because the other families must be able to get something, too."

Language barrier

Few NGOs operating in Haiti after the earthquake had Creole-speaking representatives. Response teams came from around the world, and the language barrier was a very real problem. An early task for many agencies was to provide workers with Creole phrase books so that they could communicate in the most basic way with those they were trying to help. At the same time, a computer-based translator was developed as quickly as possible.

Clean water

The need for clean drinking water was even more desperate. Haiti is a hot country, and the air was filled with dust from the concrete. Water mains were broken and water was contaminated. People needed clean water for drinking, washing wounds, and washing their bodies and clothes. Using dirty water would cause illness.

The U.S. aircraft carrier *Carl Vinson* arrived in Haiti at dawn on January 15. During the day, it delivered 29,000 gallons (132,000 liters) of fresh water. The ship can **distill** 330,000 gallons (1.5 million liters) of water a day— a valuable supply to Haiti. It delivered 600,000 emergency food rations and 100,000 2-gallon (10-liter) water containers.

Frustration

Delivering food, water, and medical supplies was difficult. Roads were blocked and damaged, and organization was poor. Jan Egerland of the UN said: "Days three, four, and five are the most frustrating. Everybody knows the whole world is **mobilizing**...But it takes time to reach the **beneficiaries**. The **infrastructure** has either gone or is totally clogged up." Eric Klein, head of the relief agency CAN-DO, complained: "It's terrible...There are medical supplies just sitting at the...airport."

Despair leads to crime

In some areas, desperate people looted stores and even attacked aid convoys. On January 17, Haitian police opened fire on hundreds of rioters and looters. Several countries, including the United States and Canada, sent troops to help keep order. Aid distribution trucks were accompanied by armed UN guards. Local man Leon Meleste said: "People are hungry, thirsty. They are left on their own. It is increasingly dangerous."

Think about this

Would you loot to survive? Haitian-American law professor Guy-Uriel Charles disagrees with the use of the word "looter" to describe someone reduced to stealing food to survive: "You survived the earthquake...It is now a week after, and you have eaten little or nothing...There is nowhere to buy food...people are starving, including your only surviving child. You would rather pay, or wait for aid supplies, but can't wait any longer. So you steal enough food for a few days. Are you a looter?"

The rural perspective

"We have seen no rescues here, no help at all. People are dying of starvation, even the survivors. We have nothing, we need help. We welcome the [relief workers] with open arms. We hoped they would come."

Jean Ky Louis, store worker in Léogâne

Outside the city

Although attention focused on Port-au-Prince, the impact outside the city was just as great—and sometimes greater. With many roads broken up or blocked by landslides, rural areas were completely cut off.

The town of Léogâne was closer to the earthquake's epicenter than Port-au-Prince, and 80 to 90 percent of its buildings were destroyed. Around 30,000 people (out of the town's population of 134,000) died.

The first rescue team arrived in Léogâne on January 17, five days after the earthquake. When more aid arrived, it was brought by small private planes, which landed on the road. By February 4, 320 flights had come into Léogâne carrying nearly 370,000 pounds (168,000 kilograms) of cargo and 1,580 passengers, mostly doctors and missionaries.

Domino effects

Around 600,000 people left Port-au-Prince in the days after the earthquake, many going to relatives in the countryside. Food prices went up, and farming families had to spend their savings on food. Many ate the seeds they were saving to plant for the 2010 crop, or they killed and ate their goats. Goats are farmed for milk and meat, but this only works if female goats are kept for breeding and not slaughtered.

Pedestrians walk past scenes of devastation on a street in Léogâne.

DOSSIER:
THE USNS *COMFORT*

The ship USNS *Comfort* is a **hospital ship** that was sent to Haiti from Washington, D.C., to provide care for injured patients. The *Comfort* is a mobile hospital for military and relief operations, and it is also used for charitable work, helping children born with deformities. It arrived at the Port-au-Prince sea port on January 19, 2010, and immediately began receiving patients referred by other hospitals and clinics. It left Haiti on February 27.

QUICK FACTS

NUMBER OF BEDS:	Around 1,000
NUMBER OF INTENSIVE CARE BEDS:	Usually 60, but increased to 80 for the Haiti mission
NUMBER OF OPERATING ROOMS:	12
PATIENT CARE:	Many delivered by helicopter after a trauma surgeon and doctor assessed them on land

The USNS *Comfort* is a hospital ship.

Health care

More than 300,000 people were injured in the earthquake, but only one hospital was left operational. Aid agencies set up portable hospitals and clinics, but medical supplies and workers were hard to come by, and all clinics were overstretched. Often, patients had to lie outside as the hospital tents were filled to overflowing. Some patients were turned away.

Emergency shelter

The earthquake left about 1.5 million people homeless. At first, many people slept outside. International aid organizations soon provided temporary shelters in the form of tents or simple **tarps** that could be held up with sticks, and these were often grouped in camps. Ricardo, a young father in Port-au-Prince, described his shelter: "Our house was completely destroyed. But we were lucky; some relatives and friends were killed. For the first two weeks, we lived under sheets and blankets strung from wooden poles."

The aid worker's perspective

Ruth Mlay, a program officer from WorldVision Australia, visited a hospital in Mirebalais, north of Port-au-Prince, on January 15:

"Haitians...are teeming [pouring] in from the capital in search of medical support, water, and food. The only hospital was full to capacity and...they soon ran out of simple first aid supplies—I had to pull my first-aid kit out of my bag and hand it to them. We gave the hospital our supplies of water, juice, and anything else we had."

Poor sanitation and overcrowding in camps led to disease. Cholera, a disease spread through dirty drinking water, appeared in October 2010 in Haiti and became the worst outbreak in modern times. In the first three years, over 8,000 people died.

Camp life

Camps sprang up quickly. Tents were crowded together, leaving people with little privacy and no security. At first, there was no running water or proper sewage drainage in the huge tent cities. But it made relief work easier to have survivors living in recognized camps. Aid agencies built latrines, provided medical care, and distributed the available food and water.

Short-term solution

The shelters were not strong enough to last long. NGOs started to build **transitional housing** in the camps, where people could live while waiting for permanent houses to be built. These offered a better standard of living, but survivors were stuck in the shacks for years, since they were no longer an urgent priority. Some people thought that the transitional shelters simply replaced the old slums with new slums.

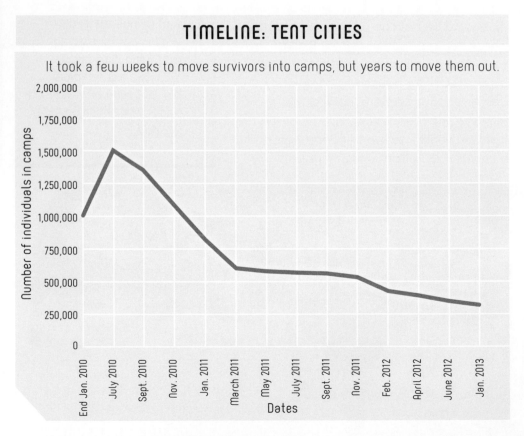

TIMELINE: TENT CITIES

It took a few weeks to move survivors into camps, but years to move them out.

Trouble brewing

Although they were desperately needed, the camps had problems. They were often badly run, underfunded, and overcrowded. The stress and boredom of camp life made people angry, and many camps were **plagued** by crime and violent gangs. Patrols and floodlights were introduced to keep people safe at night. Camp manager Richard Poole said: "My three months at [camp] Corail were one of the most difficult periods I have experienced in my 30 years as a humanitarian worker."

People outside the camps were also unhappy. The Place Boyer camp was in a previously wealthy commercial district of Port-au-Prince. The stench of dirty water and filthy toilets made the camp unpopular. One businessman complained: "These people are losing us customers; they shouldn't be here. What's more, they have no money to spend and buy nothing from us."

But the homeless people had no choice. One resident said, "I'm waiting for a home. As soon as I get one, I'll leave—and it's the same for everyone in the camp. Since they don't want us here, they'll be forced to give us somewhere to live. Because they're not going to kill us, are they? The **dictatorship** in Haiti is over. Today, it's a democracy!"

Scientists at Work

Earth's crust is divided into large "plates" of land, known as **tectonic plates**, that fit together like a jigsaw puzzle and move very slowly. Haiti lies on the **fault line** between the North American plate and the Caribbean plate. Friction prevents the plates from moving smoothly, and tension builds up as they get stuck. When the tension is too great, the plates jolt, causing an earthquake. The energy this creates can escape in a series of small earthquakes or a single large one. It is impossible to tell which it will be.

Monitoring the moving Earth

Earthquake scientists monitor movement of Earth's crust using instruments called **seismometers** at different locations around the planet. By comparing the information with past records, they try to predict where earthquakes might happen. However, this is an imprecise science. There were no warning shocks to show that the Haiti earthquake was coming—just the extreme readings from seismometers in Haiti, sent to the USGS automatically over the Internet while the earthquake was happening.

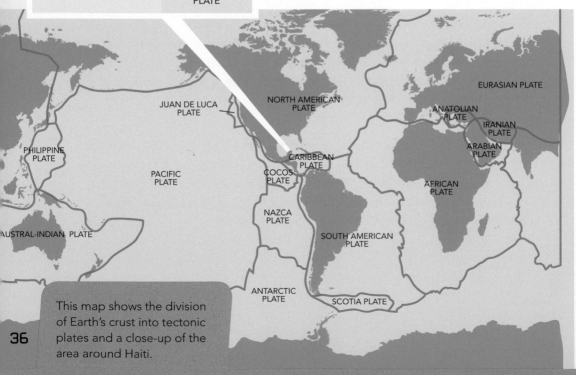

This map shows the division of Earth's crust into tectonic plates and a close-up of the area around Haiti.

The magnitude of an earthquake is given by a number 1.0 to 10.0, indicating the amount of energy released by the earthquake. The Haiti earthquake had a magnitude of 7.0. The strongest recorded earthquake was magnitude 9.5 in Chile in 1960. The magnitude scale is **logarithmic**, so an earthquake of magnitude 7.0 is 10 times as powerful as one of magnitude 6.0.

Magnitude is not the only thing that affects the amount of shaking an earthquake causes. The depth of an earthquake's epicenter is also very important. The Haiti earthquake was very shallow, and the amount of shaking that occurred was greater than many deeper earthquakes of the same magnitude. In addition, the kind of rock or soil under a place can also affect the amount of shaking. Port au Prince is built on river and flood sediments (or relatively loose rocks), which shook like jelly during the earthquake.

TIMELINE:
MAJOR SHOCKS

JAN. 12, 2010, 4:53 p.m.
Magnitude 7.0 (main earthquake)

5:00 p.m.
Magnitude 6.0

5:12 p.m.
Magnitude 5.0

Jan. 20, 2010, 6:03 a.m.
Magnitude 5.9

Total of 59 aftershocks by February 23, 2010

The scientist's perspective

"[The fault line Haiti lies on] has been locked solid for about the last 250 years. It's been gathering stress all that time as the plates move past each other, and it was really just a matter of time before it released all that energy."

Dr. Roger Musson, scientist

The deadliest earthquake

The worst earthquake ever was in Shaanxi, China, in 1556. It was 30 times as powerful as the Haiti earthquake. It killed 830,000 people and destroyed an area 500 miles (804 kilometers) wide.

"Mountains and rivers changed places and roads were destroyed...the ground suddenly rose up and formed new hills, or it sank abruptly and became new valleys."

Contemporary account, 1556

New maps

Immediately after the earthquake, images from several satellites were used to make emergency maps of the area. These images showed how the ground had changed. The maps helped response teams to see where the impact was greatest, to plan passable routes for delivering relief, and to identify areas that would be suitable for setting up relief camps.

Satellites produce both aerial photographs of the area and **radar imagery**. Radar can "see" through cloud and dust cover and can also identify possible hazards, such as landslides that can be triggered by earthquakes. The first post-disaster maps were ready on January 14.

Tsunami or no tsunami?

Earthquakes can be followed by a tsunami—a great wave produced by disruption to the sea that washes over the land, causing even more destruction. A warning was issued after the Haiti earthquake, but although four people were drowned by a small surge, the feared tsunami did not occur. By contrast, the Tohoku earthquake in Japan in 2011 was followed by a tsunami that caused many more deaths than the original earthquake.

Huge tented cities provided shelter for people made homeless by the earthquake.

DOSSIER:
CHILE, FEBRUARY 27, 2010

An earthquake of magnitude 8.8 struck Chile on February 27, 2010, six weeks after the Haiti earthquake. The epicenter was just off the coast. The quake was followed by a series of aftershocks, up to magnitude 6.9. Soon after the quake, scientists installed seismometers in the area and measured 20,000 aftershocks in six months. Casualties were much lower than in Haiti, because the quake did not strike a densely populated area, and buildings in Chile were built to withstand earthquakes.

QUICK FACTS

MAGNITUDE: 500 times more powerful than the Haiti earthquake

CASUALTIES: 523 people dead, 24 missing, 9 percent lost their homes

LOOTING: Food and essential items, but also household and luxury goods

AID: Chile handled humanitarian aid alone, launching a "telethon" that raised $58 million—double its target—in 24 hours

∧ This bridge in Santiago, Chile, was brought down by the earthquake in February 2010.

Watching for the future

Scientists examined radar satellite data to investigate the **deformation** of the land. Using data from the earthquake, they figured out the likelihood of future major earthquakes. Roger Musson of the **British Geological Survey** summed up their findings: "The pressure has probably shifted to the west, so it's likely that there will be another earthquake or perhaps a succession of earthquakes moving westward [from Haiti] to Jamaica. That is not in the immediate future but in the next decades or 100 years. My guess would be that we will have another earthquake in Haiti or Jamaica within 20 or 40 years."

Lessons from Haiti

The devastation in Haiti prompted scientists to investigate the risks to cities built on or near fault lines. The combination of a large, overcrowded population and poorly constructed buildings led to the high death toll. Special scientists who study hazards compiled a list of cities that would also suffer high death rates in the event of an earthquake, due to badly built buildings and cramped living conditions.

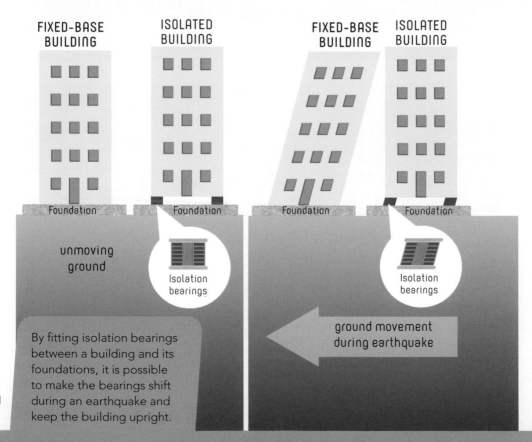

FIXED-BASE BUILDING   ISOLATED BUILDING   FIXED-BASE BUILDING   ISOLATED BUILDING

Foundation   Foundation   Foundation   Foundation

unmoving ground

Isolation bearings

Isolation bearings

By fitting isolation bearings between a building and its foundations, it is possible to make the bearings shift during an earthquake and keep the building upright.

ground movement during earthquake

Cities that would be most seriously affected by a 6.0 magnitude earthquake, with estimated deaths			
1	Kathmandu	Nepal	69,000 (population 1 million)
2	Istanbul	Turkey	55,000 (population 10 million)
3	Delhi	India	38,000 (population 1.8 million)
4	Quito	Ecuador	15,000 (population 1 million)
5	Manila	Philippines	13,000 (population 1.6 million)
6	Islamabad/ Rawalpindi	Pakistan	12,500 (population 1 million)
7	San Salvador	El Salvador	11,500 (population 2.2 million)
7	Mexico City	Mexico	11,500 (population 8.8 million)
7	Izmir	Turkey	11,500 (population 3.5 million)
10	Jakarta	Indonesia	11,000 (population 18.4 million)

This shows the city of Kathmandu in Nepal. If a serious earthquake struck, 69,000 of the population of 1 million could die.

Relief to Recovery

There was a lot to do in Haiti. The buildings needed to be rebuilt, but so did people's lives and communities.

Toward rebuilding

Before any construction work could start in Haiti, there were millions of tons of rubble to move—enough to fill 4,000 Olympic swimming pools—and more unsafe buildings to demolish. One year after the earthquake, only 20 percent of the rubble had been removed.

Jessica Faieta of the UN in Haiti admitted, "There hasn't really been a strategy for debris clearance." It was difficult to clear the land for a number of reasons. People already using the land were unwilling to move. It was also almost impossible to find out who owned the land. "How can you build a house for someone when you don't know that someone else won't turn up and claim the land?" asked Julie Schindall of Oxfam.

Making progress

Although progress is very slow, there have been some success stories. Some agencies have built new homes, using construction methods that will make them safe in the event of another earthquake. Sarah Marsh of the charity CAFOD said: "We believe it's crucial to build back better—to make sure that new homes are far more solidly built than the ones they are replacing…That's why we've tested the design of all the houses we've built."

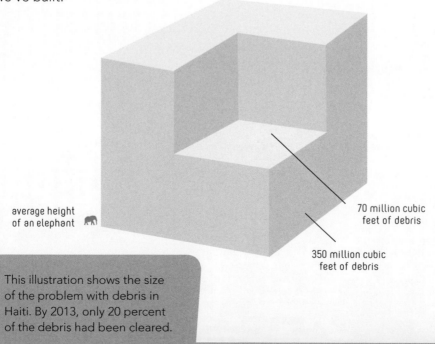

average height of an elephant

70 million cubic feet of debris

350 million cubic feet of debris

This illustration shows the size of the problem with debris in Haiti. By 2013, only 20 percent of the debris had been cleared.

A construction expert's view

"There are tents blocking streets and in some areas you just have footpaths between buildings, making it difficult to access with heavy machinery...I have been in this kind of work for 30 years all over the world, and I have not yet experienced anything of this complexity...To rebuild a capital city that was not in good shape before will take many years."

Michael Wyrick, the Haiti Recovery Group

A nursery worker's view

"The real solution is for the buildings to be rebuilt properly, with the right materials and the necessary infrastructure to withstand earthquakes. After that there has to be investment in two key areas: education and health. That, and ensuring that we can all eat every day."

Marlene Richard, a nurse who worked in a nursery that was destroyed in the earthquake

Ideally, aid money should be spent on those who need it most, but only 1 percent of donations were spent within Haiti—the rest went to foreign contractors, most of them American. Haiti has received about 15 to 21 percent of the longer-term relief aid. Sarah Marsh said:

"We believe it's vital that Haitians lead the recovery. While some aid agencies have flown in foreign contractors to build houses, we've worked with local Haitian engineers and trained local people to be masons [builders]. When I've watched people being trained, it's been clear how motivated they are to learn new skills so that they can play a role in the **reconstruction** effort."

New jobs

For Haiti to recover from the disaster, people needed jobs. One way of getting people back to work is to employ them in relief and recovery work. Some Haitians took jobs in the camps and some worked on building temporary shelters or new homes, hospitals, and schools.

Another way to help people to become self-supporting is through business **grants**. Oxfam was one of many charities that provided small grants to Haitians to start or build a business. The money can be used to buy supplies, equipment, or even chickens. It helped many Haitians to get back on their feet.

Think about this

How would you prioritize building and housing needs? Which are the most important buildings to rebuild? How would you decide who should be moved first into new homes and who should stay in a camp?

First Aid
PREMYE SWEN

Block 1
Houses
101-108

People work to build new houses near Léogâne.

Desert's story: The carpenter

Desert Jean Daniel worked in Port-au-Prince as a carpenter before the earthquake. His house was destroyed, and he ended up in a tent camp. When the Red Cross began to build transitional shelters, Desert got a job as a carpenter helping to make them.

"It's very important to have people from the community helping to build the homes. It makes sure that people are invested in their work, and it also brings money to the camp."

Desert was able to use his skills, earn money, and help his community.

A new home: The Polinius' story

"We just started building a shelter, using whatever material we had, including getting trees and covering them with mud. We've been living here, in this hut, nearly two years. We didn't move anywhere after the earthquake."

Madame Polinius, whose house was destroyed in the earthquake

When WorldVision provided building materials for more permanent shelter, Madame Polinius and her husband helped out:

"We brought materials from the distribution site for them, and took care of their equipment. When the staff was working on the new shelter, we made coffee for them, food, carried materials, brought water, and helped to mix concrete."

Money problems

Not everyone was happy with the way charities and NGOs distributed lifestyle aid. Auguste Gregory runs a telephone-charging business in a camp. He explained that a program that gave grants of up to $1,000 to some small businesses, but not to all, led to problems: "The NGOs divided us. People fought with each other. Some people went to prison. Others went into hiding."

Three years after the disaster, President Michel Martelly said, "We don't just want the money to come to Haiti. Stop sending money. Let's fix it. Let's fix it." He felt that money alone could not help Haiti. A spirit of international cooperation was needed, with an investment of time for figuring out what was needed and how to deliver it properly.

Rebuilding lives

Many people in Haiti had lost everything, including their loved ones. Many had psychological wounds that would be hard to heal. Some of them were also physically scarred. Rebuilding meant adjusting to their losses and finding a way to go on living. The 16-year-old blogger Krizkadiak explained how her priorities changed:

> "You can't think the same way you used to, you're not allowed to have the same priorities as you did before…Now you know what really counts in life…loving your brother more than anything, having the people you care about close to you…or simply being alive, being able to eat, sleep…nothing else."

Healing with soccer: The coach and the player

Franz runs a soccer program in Cité Soleil called Soccer for Life, funded by Mercy Corps. One of the players is Emmanuella. She was indoors when the earthquake struck and was trapped when cement fell on her.

> "I saw people who had died. I was afraid because I thought I was going to die. After the earthquake, I lived in a tent with my mother. We didn't have a bed. We made beds with bricks…I am often afraid because sometimes there is killing and violence."

Emmanuella's father was murdered. She was very depressed when Franz included her in Soccer for Life, but now she loves the game: "Playing soccer makes me happy."

Franz gave his side of the story: "Emmanuella was not well at all. Soccer is one of the tools we use to help the children forget a lot of things and live together in harmony…Emmanuella's life turned around. I can see that soccer can bring the change that we want in Cité Soleil."

Orphans

One terrible result of the earthquake was that a large number of children were orphaned or separated from their parents. Haiti already had a huge problem with orphaned and abandoned children. After the earthquake, the authorities had to be very careful that lone children were not abused or taken illegally. The legal orphanages were overflowing, and many foreigners were eager to adopt children. But proper procedures had to be kept in order to protect the children. A group of U.S. missionaries was stopped when it tried to take 33 children out of Haiti.

Healing minds

The psychological trauma that affected people who lived through the quake was hard to deal with. Some people did not heal and have permanent mental health problems. But trying to rebuild a sense of normality helped many. Aid workers and Haitians worked together using art, music, sports, and **psychotherapy** to help depressed and traumatized people. Working with young people was particularly important, as they are Haiti's future.

Haitian artist Raymond Bauduy has moved from painting the countryside to painting scenes of the earthquake in the city.

What Have We Learned?

It remains very difficult to predict earthquakes, and scientists have not found any other methods to do this since Haiti. For now, all we can do is learn how to deal with them better.

Preparing for next time

The poor quality of buildings in Haiti was the main cause of the high death toll. Haiti now has regulations to control new buildings so that they can withstand earthquakes and hurricanes. According to Steven Rottman of the University of California, Los Angeles, "The mantra [slogan] of disaster recovery is not to put it back the way it was before it happened, but to make it better and more resistant to subsequent hazards."

Earthquake drill

In Japan, many schools have regular earthquake drills to prepare children. They practice the "drop and cover" method:
- Drop to the floor where you are—don't try to go outside.
- Cover yourself by hiding under a strong table—don't stand in a doorway.
- Hold on to something stable until the shaking stops.

However, there is more to planning for the future than simply hoping to make safer buildings. The Disasters Emergency Committee (DEC) coordinates the relief efforts of different organizations. In its report on the Haiti earthquake, it said that as more people live in **urban** areas, the needs of disaster zones have changed. It recommended new approaches, such as working with street-food vendors to make sure everyone has access to safe food. Another lesson DEC took from Haiti is that although long-term camps looked like a good idea at the time, they failed to create proper communities and became new slums.

Haiti's lessons

The lessons of Haiti can help us anticipate and deal with future disasters:

- Natural disasters are unpredictable. We sometimes know where they are likely to strike, but not when. There will always be surprises.

- Even the emergency services are affected by a big disaster. This leaves an area without effective health care and policing, and sometimes without effective government.

- People affected by a disaster have immediate needs and long-term needs. Both types must be met by relief work.

- People have different perspectives on events. We need to be sensitive to different points of view.

- Relief work will always encounter unexpected problems or changes, so it is important to be able to adapt to them.

- Relief efforts must be properly coordinated, and those in charge must consult local people so that actions are appropriate.

- Recovery work should involve local businesses, helping the local economy to get back on track.

> ### A professor's perspective
>
> "Is there hope for Haiti? There is a lot of hope for Haiti. It is the only country their people call 'sweetheart.'"
>
> Michelet Divers, Haitian professor of literature

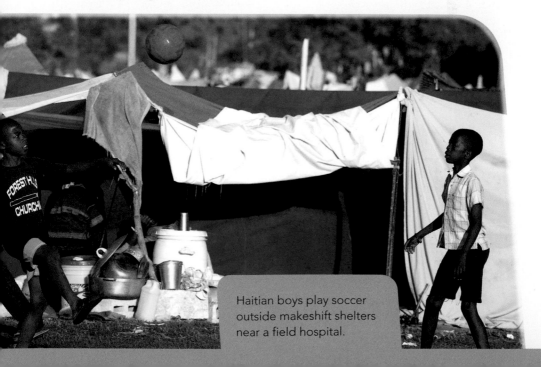

Haitian boys play soccer outside makeshift shelters near a field hospital.

Timeline

January 12, 2010	Local people try to dig family and neighbors from the rubble, but there is no official help
January 13	Haitian rescue workers take people to the only open hospital, an Argentinian military field hospital. Doctors Without Borders announces it will start operating out of two other hospitals.
	Rescue teams arrive from Peru and Cuba and start work
	U.S. Coast Guard aircraft survey the area
	U.S. Air Force staff reopen the airport and start air traffic control
	Doctors Without Borders has already treated 1,000 people
January 14	IRC begins distributing food; relief supplies flood into the airport, but distributing them is extremely difficult
	The American Red Cross raises $3 million in 24 hours with a text-message giving campaign
January 15	Arrival of USS *Carl Vinson* with water, food packs, and water containers
	Haitian airspace open only to relief flights; roads from Dominican Republic clogged
	9,000 dead bodies removed from the streets and buried or burned
	Bands of rioters and looters with machetes and guns cause chaos in parts of Port-au-Prince. People desperate for food attack aid convoys. The UN advises convoys carrying food and water to travel with armed guards.
January 16	U.S. military helicopters start dropping food and other supplies to survivors
	Casualties estimated at 200,000; 3 million need food, water, and shelter
January 17	Russian search and rescue team says it will not operate at night because of threats of violence
	Plane carrying an inflatable hospital refused landing permission in Haiti and is rerouted to the Dominican Republic, adding a 24-hour delay, as it has to come by road
January 18	U.S. Air Force begins aid drops by parachute in the countryside outside Port-au-Prince
January 19	Canadian Air Communications and Control Squadron open Jacmel airport, south of Port-au-Prince, with radar control provided by a ship in the nearby bay

January 21	There are now 40 functioning medical centers, including eight field hospitals
January 22	UN World Food Program delivers 1.2 million meals
January 23	Official end of rescue efforts Some international networks start to broadcast in Creole in Haiti
January 31	Major UN distribution of food aid starts in Port-au-Prince. Only women with families have vouchers and are allowed to collect food—55 pounds (25 kilograms) of rice. UN soldiers guard the distribution.
February	Electricity and street lighting restored to parts of Port-au-Prince
February 1	Border authorities prevent the illegal export of 33 children by a religious group, the New Life Children's Refuge
February 8	Last survivor pulled from the rubble
February 19	Temporary seismometer network set up in Haiti to monitor ground conditions
February 22	Commercial flights resume from Port-au-Prince airport
February 23	President René Préval announces it will take three years to clear rubble
June 30	About 98 percent of rubble in Port-au-Prince still not moved
September 30	More than 1 million people still live in tents
October	Cholera outbreak starts; it will kill over 8,200 in Haiti and nearby countries over the coming months and years
2013	Total aid payments to Haiti reach $9 billion. Only 1 percent of humanitarian aid has been spent within Haiti. They have received 15 to 21 percent of longer-term relief aid.

Glossary

aftershock tremors that occur after the main impact of an earthquake

beneficiary person who benefits from a gift, usually of money or aid

British Geological Survey organization that provides advice and information about earth sciences

corruption abuse of a system by paying bribes or making threats in order to get something to happen

damage-assessment team group of experts who figure out how serious the damage is in an area and its impact and implications

deformation distortion or displacement of the ground as a result of earthquake activity

democracy political system in which the people in a society elect their leaders

dictatorship political system in which a single leader takes charge, often by force

distill heat mixed liquids and then cool to separate different liquids or remove one

donate give money or a gift, often to a charity, to help those in need

epicenter point on Earth's surface directly above the place where an earthquake occurs underground

expatriate person who has left the country he or she was born in to live in another country

fault line where two or more tectonic plates meet; where earthquakes are likely to occur

field hospital temporary hospital set up at the site of an emergency or battle

grant money given to a person or organization to do something specific, such as start a business

graphic containing explicit images that might be upsetting

hemisphere half (of Earth)

Holocaust episode during World War II in which Nazi Germany imprisoned and executed large groups of people, including Jews, Romany, disabled people, and homosexuals

hospital ship ship equipped to operate as a hospital

humanitarian someone who prioritizes the rights or interests of people

hydraulic jack equipment used to move or lift heavy weights

infrastructure buildings, roads, power supplies, and other basic structures and facilities needed for the operation of a society or business

latrine simple toilet, sometimes just a trench or hole in the ground used as a toilet

logarithmic displaying intervals in a scale that relate to orders of magnitude (1, 10, 100) rather than simple linear intervals (1, 2, 3)

loot steal from a damaged or empty property

magnitude describes the energy released during an earthquake—for example, magnitude 7.0

media radio, television, newspapers, magazines, and the Internet

missionary person working in a community to grow or spread a religion

mobilize put something into motion

morgue place where bodies are kept until they are identified, autopsied, or released for burial

nongovernment organization (NGO) nonprofit organization that is not part of a national government and pursues a social or political goal. Examples include the United Nations, Red Cross, and Doctors Without Borders.

open-source software software that can be freely copied, adapted, and distributed

plagued subjected to something to the point that it becomes troublesome

psychotherapy treatment for mental illness, such as depression, or a trauma, such as death, illness, or surviving or witnessing a disaster

radar imagery images produced from interpreting how radar (electromagnetic waves) bounces off surfaces

reconnaissance visiting or exploring an area to gather information about it

reconstruction rebuilding

republic country that has a nominated or elected leader rather than a king or queen

sanitary item item relating to hygiene

search and rescue team group of people, and often dogs, who locate and rescue those who are trapped in confined spaces, usually as a result of a disaster

seismometer equipment that measures the movement of the ground

slum area of poor quality housing, often badly built and inhabited by people living in poverty

tarp thick sheet, often of plastic or canvas, used as a protective covering

tectonic plate piece of Earth's crust that covers Earth like a cracked eggshell

transitional housing shelters intended for people to live in for a short period while permanent houses are built

tremor shaking or vibrating movement, as in an earthquake

United Nations (UN) international organization of countries aiming to promote peace and cooperation throughout the world

urban relating to a city or town

U.S. Coast Guard organization that patrols the shores, rescues people and ships in danger at sea, helps to fight crime at sea, and assists in disasters

U.S. Geological Survey (USGS) organization that provides advice and information about earth sciences

void space or gap

voodoo set of religious beliefs followed by some people in the Caribbean. Central to voodoo is the belief that god (Bondye) does not take an active part in human lives, but people can gain help by praying to various spirits.

Find Out More

Nonfiction books

Dwyer, Helen. *Earthquakes!* (Eyewitness Disaster). New York: Marshall Cavendish Benchmark, 2011.

Green, Jen. *Earthquake* (Emergency). Mankato, Minn.: Arcturus, 2012.

Rooney, Anne. *Responding to Emergencies* (Charities in Action). Chicago: Heinemann LIbrary, 2013.

Fiction book

Lake, Nick. *In Darkness*. New York: Bloomsbury, 2012.

Web sites

www.dropcoverholdon.org
This web site tells you how to prepare for an earthquake.

www.whitehouse.gov/haitiearthquake
Learn more about the U.S. response to the earthquake in Haiti at this official White House site, which includes videos.

www.who.int/hac/crises/hti/en/
This WHO web site includes links to information and updates about the earthquake in Haiti and its aftermath.

www.youtube.com/playlist?list=PL4F3959441305AAA3
This is a playlist of the United Nations' video footage of the Haiti earthquake and its aftermath.

Apps

QuakeWatch, LateNightProjects (iPad/iPhone)
This app shows all earthquake activity around the world as it happens.

QuakeZones Pro, AppDudes (iPad/iPhone)
This provides a massive database of earthquakes through history, as well as updates on current earthquake activity.

Topics to research

You might like to research any of the following topics to increase your knowledge about the earthquake in Haiti and how it fits into the context of earth sciences.

1. Tectonics: Earth's crust is divided into large slabs that slowly move around. Their movement and interactions are responsible for earthquakes and volcanic eruptions, and also for the slowly changing shape and position of the continents.

2. Disaster relief: The Haiti earthquake produced a worldwide response. Other types of natural and human-made disasters produce responses that are in some ways similar and in other ways different. Find out about how we respond to disasters such as extreme weather (floods, droughts, hurricanes), volcanic eruptions, landslides, wildfires, tsunamis, industrial accidents, and wars.

3. Haiti: The country has had a turbulent past with political difficulties as well as previous earthquakes. Find out about the history of the island and how modern-day Haiti emerged.

Index